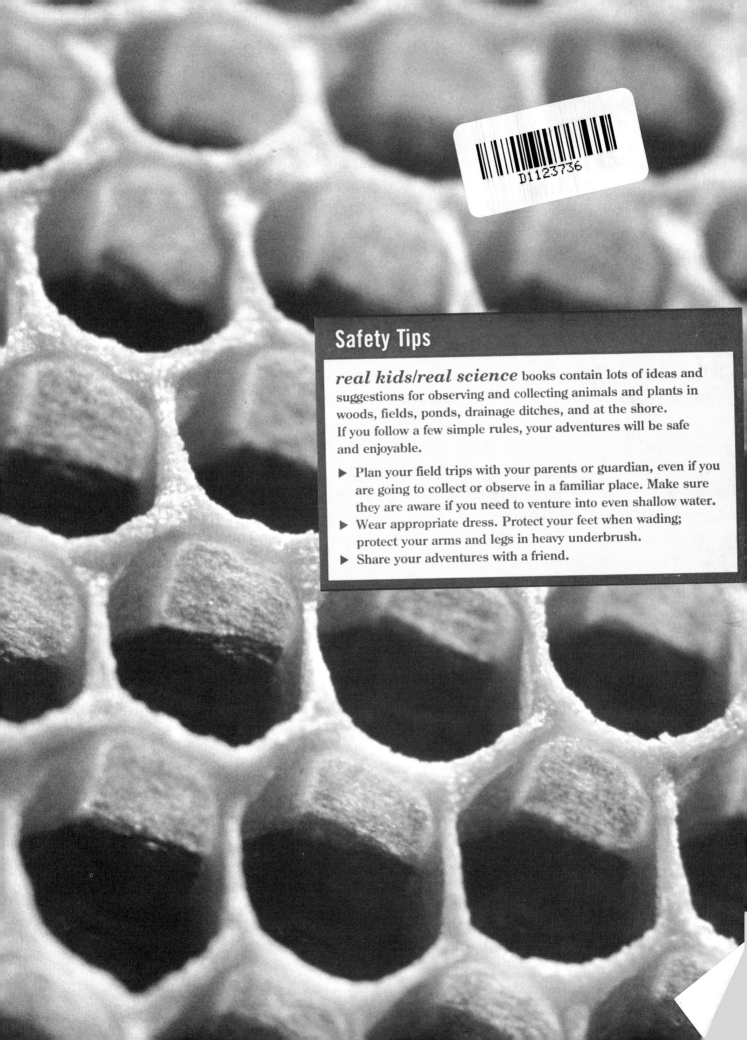

D1123736

Safety Tips

real kids/real science books contain lots of ideas and
suggestions for observing and collecting animals and plants in
woods, fields, ponds, drainage ditches, and at the shore.
If you follow a few simple rules, your adventures will be safe
and enjoyable.

▶ Plan your field trips with your parents or guardian, even if you
  are going to collect or observe in a familiar place. Make sure
  they are aware if you need to venture into even shallow water.
▶ Wear appropriate dress. Protect your feet when wading;
  protect your arms and legs in heavy underbrush.
▶ Share your adventures with a friend.

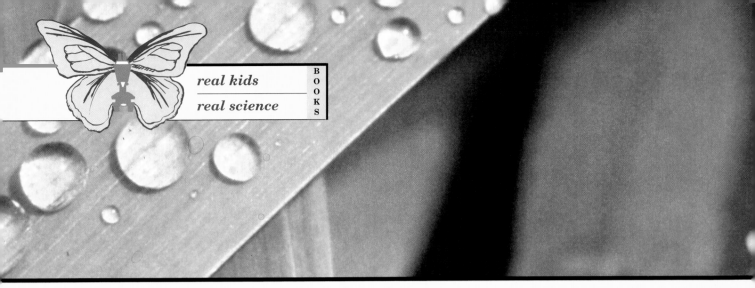

Entomology

"Study nature, not books." —LOUIS AGASSIZ

real kids
real science

BOOKS

Entomology

written by Ellen Doris
original photography by Len Rubenstein

PRODUCED IN ASSOCIATION WITH

The Children's School of Science
Woods Hole, Massachusetts

THAMES AND HUDSON

What is this book about?

This is not only a book about insects. This is a book about Entomology, which is the study of insects. In it you will find projects, field trips, ideas, and suggestions. They will help you to explore the insect kingdom yourself.

How to use this book

Entomology is organized as a collection of separate experiments, investigations, and discoveries. It shows you where to look for insects, and how to study them once you find them. Though some basic terms and concepts are introduced in the first few sections, you don't have to follow the book step by step from beginning to end. We suggest you browse through it first. Look for a field trip that's easy to do near your home. Or perhaps you'll want to raise crickets because you know where you can find them. Also, this book will be a lot more fun if you share some of the projects and field trips with someone else, a friend, or a parent.

Where can you get specimens and subjects to study? And equipment?

First of all, try to collect them yourself. And adapt equipment that you already have at home, like an old aquarium. But, you'll be surprised to find how many live samples can be ordered from biological supply houses at pretty reasonable costs. They also sell equipment like nets and special pins for displaying insects. There is a list of equipment and specimens on page 62, but don't feel you have to order all of it at once. Except for a net, you'll be surprised at how much you can find and adapt yourself.

What is an imago? And how do you pronounce Oncopeltus fasciatus?

Check out the Glossary on page 63, which defines all terms that are printed in bold type. But don't get bogged down trying to pronounce long Latin names; sound them out as best as you can and go on.

Think for yourself

You'll probably have to adapt some of the projects you find in this book. You may not live near a field, or a pond, but you can search for similar things in drainage ditches and vacant lots. You may not find the same caterpillars to raise that the kids at the Science School found, but try the same project with another caterpillar. Remember, not every project works according to plan. Sometimes at the School, for instance, the caterpillars we raise never emerge from their cocoons or chryssalises. Think about why—was the room too hot? too cold? and try again.

The Children's School of Science
Woods Hole, Massachusetts

Each summer, in an old-fashioned school-house whose rooms are crowded with plants, nets, microscopes, and bubbling aquaria, several hundred children between the ages of seven and sixteen attend classes for two hours each morning. Led by teachers who are experts in their field, the children take frequent field trips and work with each other on projects and experiments. The classes are informal, and courses range from Seashore Exploration to Ornithology to Neurobiology. For over seventy-five years, this remarkable institution has fostered the joy of discovery by encouraging direct observation of natural phenomena.

Contents

This book is dedicated to the teachers and students of the Children's School of Science, without whose enthusiastic help it would not have been possible.

Copyright © 1993 Thames and Hudson Inc., New York
First published in the United States in 1993 by Thames and Hudson Inc.,
500 Fifth Avenue, New York, New York 10110

Photos copyright © Len Rubenstein unless otherwise indicated.

Library of Congress Catalog Card Number 92-62479

Designed, typeset, and produced by Beth Tondreau Design ■ Managing Editor, Jeanne-Marie Perry

Color separations made by The Sarabande Press ■ Printed and bound in Malaysia

Introduction

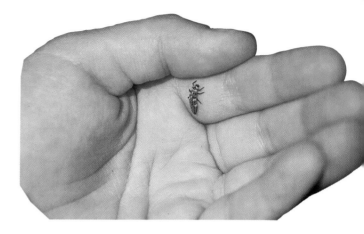

From the bees that provide us with honey and wax to the cockroaches that share our crumbs, insects amaze us, pester us, and help us to survive. Scientists have described and studied close to one million different kinds, or **species**, of insects. This makes insects the largest **class** of animals on earth, larger than all the other groups of animals combined! Scientists are still discovering new insects. They believe there are thousands more to be found, so keep your eyes open!

There are insects wherever you go. Indoors, out-of-doors, underground, underwater; they have colonized nearly every part of the earth. Almost any place is a good place to start studying them. **Entomology** is the study of insects, and this book will help you become an entomologist.

A group of animals containing a million or so different species is bound to display some diversity. We recognize a swallowtail butterfly by its beautifully patterned wings, while most of the ants we see have no wings and never fly. Grasshoppers are active in the daytime; many moths are active at night. Fully grown giant water bugs devour prey as large as tadpoles, frogs, and fish, while adult mayflies have undeveloped mouthparts and do not eat at all. When body form and behavior are so variable, how can you tell if you're looking at an insect?

This butterfly and this wasp have a lot in common, though they look very different. They are different species in the class of insects.

The basic body plan

All insects have **segmented bodies** made up of many small sections.

Insects have three major body divisions, the **head, thorax,** and **abdomen.** Mouthparts, eyes, and antennae are found on the head, while legs and wings grow from the thorax. In some insects these body divisions are easy to see. In others they are not so apparent.

The wings of this beetle cover its abdomen, but when you turn it over, segments are visible on its underside.

7

Segments are easy to see on the body of this monarch caterpillar. Can you distinguish this caterpillar's jointed legs from other appendages?

All insects have **exoskeletons,** or hard skins on the outside of their bodies. The exoskeleton gives an insect shape, gives muscles a place to attach to, protects internal organs, and keeps moist internal structures from drying out. An insect's exoskeleton does not grow. As the rest of the insect's body grows, a new skin begins to form under the old one. When the insect **molts,** the old skin splits and the insect crawls out. The soft, new exoskeleton expands at first, but once it has dried and hardened, it will not grow any larger. Some newly molted insects eat their old skins; others just leave them behind.

All insects have three pairs of **jointed legs.** Many insects have other leg-like structures projecting from their bodies as well, so simply counting what look like legs may not be enough to separate insects from other, similar looking, animals.

These stink bug eggs were found on a tree leaf.

An Insect Checklist

✓ segmented bodies
✓ exoskeletons
✓ three pairs of jointed legs
✓ eggs

If you find an animal and you can only check off one or two of these characteristics, it is probably not an insect.

This earthworm has a segmented body like insects do, but no legs or exoskeleton. It is an **annelid,** *not an insect.*

This crayfish has an exoskeleton like insects do, but it has more than six jointed legs. It is a **crustacean,** *not an insect.*

All insects develop from eggs. In a few cases, the eggs develop inside the female's body, and she gives birth to live young. Most insects, however, lay their eggs in soil or water, on plants, or even on other insects.

GETTING STARTED

The best way to learn about insects is to find one and watch it. What does it look like? How does it move? What does it do? These are questions you can answer yourself by looking.

In the field

Fields are home to many insects. When you visit a field, carefully search the stems, leaves,

and flowers of plants. You'll find bees and butterflies collecting nectar, beetles and caterpillars munching on leaves, and bugs sucking the juice out of plant stems. Look overhead. You may see dragonflies scouting for prey. Check under rocks for beetle larvae and ant nests. Listen for insects. Grasshoppers and crickets may be easier to hear than to see. Look for signs of insects, too. Some leave traces that let you know where they have been.

A garden trowel may aid your search for soil-dwelling insects.

A notebook or sketch pad and pencil will help you record and remember what you see.

Equipment

A few simple tools will help you study many different kinds of insects.

A hand lens, or magnifying glass, will help you get a more detailed look at the insects you find.

A net can help you catch insects that tend to fly away before you can study them.

An empty coffee can, jar, or clear plastic container temporarily holds an insect you may want to watch.

Using a Net

One way to use a net is to sweep it through tall stands of grass or wildflowers using short, quick strokes. Many insects will end up in the net, even though only a few were visible beforehand. Sometimes it's possible to net an insect in flight. Either way, by turning the net handle you can close the opening to prevent the insects from escaping. Look through the mesh net to see what you have caught, or gently transfer them to a container for further study. Most insects, even stinging ones, can be handled safely if you are careful. Of course, if you are allergic to bees you must avoid handling them.

Noticing changes

Return often to the same place to look for insects. Populations can change dramatically over time. Insects that are difficult to find during one visit may be common later on. Particular behavior, like courtship or egg laying, may give way to new activity. What changes in a familiar place can you notice over time?

Taxonomy

Scientists have developed various ways of classifying living things according to the similarities and differences among them. **Taxonomy** is another word for classification.

Classification

One taxonomic system groups all animals together in a large **kingdom**, the **Animalia**. This enormous kingdom can be divided into smaller groups, called **phyla**. The members of one phylum can be divided into **classes**, the classes into **orders**, orders into **families**, families into **genera**, and genera into **species**.

Animals quite different from one another can belong to the same phylum. Human beings are in the same phylum as fish, snakes, and sea squirts. Insects share a phylum with lobsters, ticks, and centipedes. As a phylum is further and further subdivided, the differences get sorted out. Members of the same family or genus have many things in common. Finally, each animal is grouped just with members of its own particular kind, or species.

Taxonomy of Familiar Animals

	HONEYBEES	LOBSTERS	PEOPLE
Kingdom:	Animalia	Animalia	Animalia
Phylum:	Arthropoda	Arthropoda	Chordata
Subphylum:	Mandibulata	Mandibulata	Vertebrata
Class:	Insecta	Crustacea	Mammalia
Order:	Hymenoptera	Decopoda	Primates
Family:	Apidae	Nephropsidae	Hominidae
Genus:	*Apis*	*Homarus*	*Homo*
Species:	*mellifera*	*americanus*	*sapiens*

What is a species?

Biologists use the word species to mean a distinct kind of living thing. Members of a particular species can mate and produce offspring like themselves. Animals that look quite different to us may, in fact, be members of the same species. For example, a German shepherd and a golden retriever look quite different. Yet both are members of the same species (*Canis familiaris*), and a shepherd can mate with a retriever and have puppies. Other organisms may look similar to us, but belong to different species. The monarch butterfly (*Danaus plexippus*) looks similar in many ways to the viceroy (*Limenitis archippus*). Both are large butterflies with orange and black patterned wings. Yet the two feed on different plants and survive cold weather differently. *D. plexippus* will not mate with *L. archippus*. Each is a distinct species.

Animal names

The same animal may be called by many names. Most people use common names. Since an animal may have several common names, and since some common names label more than one animal, scientists refer to animals by a combination of their Latin genus and species names. Though these names may seem hard to pronounce and remember, using them

cuts down on confusion. To a scientist the honeybee is *Apis mellifera*, the northern lobster is *Homarus americanus*, and we are *Homo sapiens*.

Confusing relatives: Why a spider is not an insect

Insects belong to the phylum **Arthropoda.** In addition to insects, this group contains spiders, lobsters, and many other animals that are similar in some ways to insects. Many are often confused with insects.

Spiders and **ticks** are found in many of the same places as insects, and like insects they have jointed legs and bodies that are divided

into parts. But if you look closely you will see that spiders have eight jointed legs instead of six, and only two major body parts. Adult ticks have one body part and eight legs. Both belong to the class **Arachnoidea.**

Pillbugs and **sowbugs** have segmented bodies, but more than three pairs of legs. They are isopods, and belong to the class **Crustacea,** as do crabs and lobsters.

Centipedes and **millipedes** have segmented bodies and jointed legs. Though they don't actually have hundreds or millions of legs, they do have more than the insect's six. They lack the three body divisions characteristic of insects. Centipedes are in the class **Chilopoda,** and millipedes belong to the **Diplopoda.**

11

Damselfly and darning needle are two common names for this insect.

Take a close look at the animals pictured here. See if you can tell what sets them apart from insects.

Metamorphosis

Metamorphosis is the word that describes insect growth. It means "change of form," so it's a fitting word to describe the amazing transformation from caterpillar to butterfly.

From egg to caterpillar

Female monarch butterflies lay tiny sculptured eggs on milkweed plants. Eggs are placed singly, usually on the underside of milkweed leaves. These eggs will hatch into caterpillars so small they are easy to overlook.

After eating its eggshell, the new caterpillar begins to eat milkweed. Soon it molts, and another period of eating begins. The caterpillar grows fast, and with each molt its body changes slightly. Long black antennae develop from small bumps on the head, and shorter but similar projections grow near the end of its abdomen.

Caterpillar to chrysalis

When it is about two weeks old, the caterpillar stops eating. It acts "sick," but actually its body is preparing for another molt. The caterpillar spins a small web of silk on the underside of a leaf, milkweed stem, or cage lid. Then it hangs upside down from the web with its body curved like the letter J. Though it may stay in this position

for some time, try to keep an eye on it so you can watch the unbelievable transformation from caterpillar to **chrysalis.**

Still upside down, the caterpillar begins to wriggle. Its striped skin splits, rolling back to reveal a green chrysalis, completely different from the caterpillar in color and form. The old skin, scrunched up in a ball, falls down. You may find it on a leaf below the chrysalis or on the floor of the cage.

Metamorphosis of a Viceroy Butterfly

The chrysalis is marked with black and metallic gold dots. For days it hangs by its black stem, or **cremaster.** Soon the outline and veins of the butterfly's wings become more visible, and the green covering gradually turns clear. A small white stripe appears below the cremaster on male chrysalises. Finally, the chrysalis splits open and a damp, crumpled butterfly crawls out.

The butterfly holds onto a leaf or the empty chrysalis, pumping fluid into its wings. When the wings are dry and the butterfly starts opening and closing them, you can let it go. It is ready to fly.

If you forgot to check for the white stripe on the chrysalis, you can still tell if your butterfly is a male or a female. Males have a widened black area, the **alar spot,** along a vein on each hind wing. On females this vein is a uniform width.

Adult monarchs drink nectar through a tube called a **proboscis.** Monarch caterpillars are picky eaters, feeding only on plants in the milkweed family, but monarch butterflies sip nectar from many kinds of flowers.

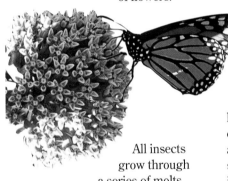

All insects grow through a series of molts, but entomologists recognize different types of metamorphosis. Butterflies, for instance, undergo **complete metamorphosis.** They hatch as tiny caterpillars, or **larvae.** Larvae pass through a number of **instars,** the stages between molts. Then they

Taxonomy

ORDER: *Lepidoptera*
 (butterflies and moths)
SUPERFAMILY:
 Papilionoidea
 (butterflies)
FAMILY: *Danaidai*
 (milkweed butterflies)
GENUS AND SPECIES:
 Danaus plexippus
 (monarch butterfly)

form a chrysalis and begin their **pupal stage.** One last change of form occurs as the adult butterfly emerges from the chrysalis. Moths, bees, flies, and beetles also have complete metamorphosis. All change from larvae to pupae before becoming adults.

Some young insects look almost like adults when they hatch. With each molt they grow a little larger, and their wings and reproductive systems develop. The young insects are called **nymphs,** and though there are a number of nymphal instars, there is no pupal stage. Entomologists call this type of development **gradual metamorphosis.** Crickets, cockroaches, cicadas, and leafhoppers are all insects with gradual metamorphosis.

13

Insect Orders

T he class **Insecta** includes a large and diverse group of animals. Scientists divide these animals into twenty-five to thirty orders. Learning the characteristics of all of these orders is a difficult task. To begin, focus on the orders that include familiar insects.

Twelve common orders are described here. As you read, think if you have ever seen an insect that fits each description. Classifying the insects you already know will help you to understand taxonomy.

An introduction to some orders of insects

The **Odonata** are dragonflies and damselflies. Adults have two pairs of large, veined wings, large eyes, and long, slender abdomens. Odonate nymphs are **aquatic,** and undergo gradual metamorphosis. The name Odonata means "tooth." Though odonates don't have actual teeth, they are impressive hunters.

Crickets, grasshoppers, locusts, praying mantids, and cockroaches make up the order **Orthoptera,**

which means "straight wings." Many insects in this order have four wings; others have two or none.

They have chewing mouthparts, and metamorphosis is gradual. The males of many species are known for the chirping sounds they make to attract mates.

Termites belong to the order **Isoptera.** These insects live in colonies in the ground or in wood, have chewing mouthparts, and gradual metamorphosis. Because some species of termites colonize houses and other wood-frame buildings, chewing away at the structural elements, termites are well known to many people.

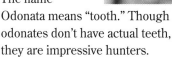

The **Dermaptera,** or earwigs, are crawling insects. Most have a pair of short, thick wings with another pair folded underneath. Dermaptera means "skin wing" and refers to the leathery front wings. The common name comes from a false belief that these insects crawl into people's ears. Earwigs have chewing mouthparts, pincer-like **cerci,** and gradual metamorphosis.

The **Anoplura** are tiny wingless insects with sucking mouthparts. They are parasites of mammals. This group includes the head lice and body lice that parasitize humans. Metamorphosis is gradual.

The **Hemiptera,** or "half wings," are aquatic and **terrestrial.** Adult bugs usually have two pairs of wings. The hind wings are membranous, and the forewings are leathery near the body and membranous away from it. When a bug is not using its wings to fly, they are folded over its body with the tips overlapping.

This creates an "X" pattern on the insect's back. Hemiptera have sucking mouthparts. Some bugs feed on plant juices, while others prey on animals. Metamorphosis is gradual.

Cicadas, leafhoppers, and aphids are some of the insects that make up the order **Homoptera.** Like the Hemiptera, they undergo gradual metamorphosis and their mouthparts are adapted for piercing and sucking. Some lack wings, while others have wings that are held in a

roof-like or tent-like fashion over their bodies when not in use. All feed on plants.

The **Coleoptera,** or "sheath-winged" insects, are the beetles. The forewings, or **elytra,** of adult beetles usually meet in the middle

of the back and cover the hind wings, forming a line or "T" pattern. Beetles undergo complete metamorphosis, with larvae that look a little like

caterpillars with hard, shiny heads. Larvae are sometimes referred to as "grubs." Both adults and larvae have chewing mouthparts. There are more species of beetles than of any other insect order.

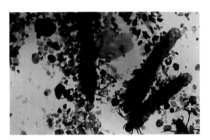

The **Trichoptera,** or caddisflies, are bound to be encountered by anyone who explores streams, lakes, or ponds. Adult caddisflies, or "Dusty Millers," look something like moths, with their wings held tent-like over their bodies. Trichoptera undergo complete metamorphosis, and larvae are aquatic. Most species construct individual homes, or cases, out of bits of vegetation, small stones, or sand grains. They drag their homes with them wherever they go.

The **Lepidoptera** include the butterflies and moths. Adults typically have four wings that are covered with tiny scales, hence the name Lepidoptera, or "scaly wings." Most adults have a long, coiled proboscis that is used to suck nectar or other liquid food. Metamorphosis is complete, and larvae, or caterpillars, have chewing mouthparts. They pupate in a chrysalis or cocoon, depending on the species.

Flies, mosquitoes, and gnats belong to the order **Diptera.** These insects have just one pair of wings, hence the name Diptera, or "two-wings." Complete metamorphosis is characteristic of this order, and larvae may be terrestrial or aquatic. Adults have sucking mouthparts, as anyone who has been bitten by a mosquito will recall.

Bees, wasps, and ants belong to the order **Hymenoptera.** The name of this order translates as "membrane-winged;" two pairs of thin, clear, membranous wings are characteristic of these insects during some phase of their life cycle. All adult bees and wasps have wings. In ants, only those that are about to mate have wings. The workers and soldiers we commonly see climbing in and out of ant hills lack them. Many female hymenoptera have a stinger or an egg-laying organ at the end of their abdomens. These insects undergo complete metamorphosis. Many hymenoptera are **social insects,** living together in colonies.

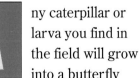

Raising Caterpillars

Any caterpillar or larva you find in the field will grow into a butterfly or moth. Caterpillars can be kept in fish tanks or large glass jars. Wire screening or cheese-cloth over the top will allow fresh air to circulate. The top should be securely fastened so the caterpillars don't escape and end up where they can't find food and water. Some stores sell large plastic boxes specially designed as "bug houses" that can be used to house a caterpillar. Caterpillar cages can also be made by shaping wire screening into a cylinder, fastening it, and adding two aluminum cake pans for the top and the bottom. Cut white paper or oaktag to fit the bottom of the cage. Insects are often easier to see against a light background.

Food

Caterpillars in captivity need plenty of fresh food; many eat at an astonishing rate. Some caterpillars are picky eaters. Monarch larvae eat only milkweed. Black swallowtail larvae feed on parsley, carrots, and related plants. Gypsy moth larvae are less particular. They seem to prefer oak leaves, but find maple, birch, beech, and cherry digestible as well. In a pinch, they'll even eat pine needles!

Take note of a caterpillar's natural surroundings before you collect it; it may be chewing away on the very plant it requires for food. If you want to keep a caterpillar that does not seem to be on its food plant, a field guide or other reference book may help you determine what it eats. If you are still unsure, it is best to release the caterpillar where you

found it once you have finished observing it. Simply filling its cage with grass or leaves may not be enough to keep your caterpillars healthy, since not all caterpillars can make use of these "foods."

Care

Keep a caterpillar's cage clean, stocked with food, and out of direct sunlight. Remove any wilted leaves or other uneaten food each day, and periodically empty feces from the bottom of the cage. Most caterpillars get water from the food they eat; you do not need to supply a bottle or dish for drinking. A few drops of water sprinkled on a leaf can be helpful, but guard against too much moisture. Dumping in a lot of damp leaves, or failing to remove old food, can create a moldy, unhealthy environment in the cage.

Time to pupate

Sooner or later your caterpillar will stop eating and be ready to pupate. It might form a chrysalis right on its food plant, as monarch caterpillars do, or spin a cocoon on a leaf or

© BILL IVY

on the side of the cage. Some caterpillars tunnel into the soil and pupate underground. Add two or three inches of moist soil to the bottom of your cage if you are raising a tunneling species. A field

guide may help you determine the needs of your particular caterpillar. If not, release it outside to pupate.

Overwintering

Some butterflies and moths have a short pupal stage and you will see adults emerge in a few weeks. When their wings are dry, let them go. Other species **overwinter** as pupae and won't emerge until spring. Keep overwintering pupae in a cool place. If there is soil in your container, check it regularly to make sure it stays a bit damp. When the weather begins to get warm, check your container daily and release any newly emerged adults.

FIELD TRIP EXPLORING A POND

I f you visit a pond in the summer, you will probably see aquatic insects right away. Dragonflies may be resting on vegetation, patrolling their territories, or searching for food. Water striders and whirligig beetles skate and spin on the water's surface. You may find mosquitoes—or they may find you.

Underwater life

Many other insects live beneath the pond's surface. If the water is clear, you can look right through it to the bottom. At first you might not see any animals, just reflections and "muck." As your eyes get accustomed to the way things look, you will begin to notice movement. What first looked like small twigs and stones turns out to be a caddisfly larva in its protective case. A bump in the mud is a dragonfly larva, quietly waiting for dinner to walk by. If the water is cloudy or overgrown with algae, sweep an aquatic net through the water to collect samples. Put your samples in a pan or bucket with water. As the sediment settles and the water clears, you can see what you have caught. You can also find aquatic insects by sifting through the bottom muck with your fingers, or looking closely at stones, sticks, and leaves you find in the water.

Other aquatic habitats

Aquatic insects can also be found in lakes, streams, rivers, ditches, and even tiny aquatic habitats like a birdbath or the standing water inside an old tire. In general, those found in still or stagnant water can be brought home for observation. Insects from streams and rivers are more difficult to rear. They often need moving water in order to get enough oxygen or food to survive.

Rearing aquatic insects

Equipment

Aquatic insects usually show up best against a light-colored background. Special pans coated with white enamel can be ordered from supply houses, or you can use old refrigerator trays. Light-colored plastic containers also work well.

Aquatic nets differ from those used to catch field insects. They are smaller and made from sturdier fabric. Many have one side flattened to fit against a stream bottom.

In cold weather

Some pond insects can be found throughout the year. Even when winter ice forms on the surface, they stay active underwater. Many species that can't survive cold temperatures as flying or terrestrial adults survive the winter as aquatic nymphs.

Most pond insects can be brought indoors and studied. You can keep them in shallow pans of water or in aquaria. If the water in your container is deep, make sure to aerate it. You will not need to supply food if you keep your insects for only a few days, but if you plan to keep them for a long period of time, be sure to collect new food for them regularly.

Carnivorous insects will hunt for other animals to eat, while herbivorous insects feed on fresh or decaying vegetation. Other insects are omnivores and will eat both plant and animal matter. Entomologists refer to some aquatic insects as detritivores, because they sift through the bottom muck, or detritus, for food.

When you are through with your study, return the animals to the same pond you collected them from. They will be able to find food there, and the temperature and chemistry of the water will suit them.

Dragonflies and Damselflies

Dragonflies and damselflies spend the first part of their lives as nymphs, underwater. You may find them crawling on aquatic plants, or in the silt and decaying vegetation on the bottom of a pond or stream. Watch for adults resting on plants or flying above the water.

Which is which?

It is easy to tell damselfly and dragonfly nymphs apart. A damselfly nymph has a long, slender body with three tail-like **gills** that allow it to "breathe" underwater. It moves through the water by wriggling from side to side. A dragonfly nymph looks more sturdy. It has a much wider abdomen with a special **gill chamber** inside. Dragonflies move, as well as breathe, by pumping water in and out of this chamber.

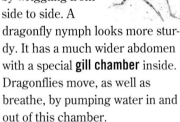

You can recognize adult damselflies by their thin, delicate bodies, and by their wings. Both pairs of wings are similar in size and shape, and the damselflies tend to tip them up or fold them parallel to their bodies when resting. Dragonflies are stockier, and their hind wings are wider near the abdomen than their forewings are. Dragonflies usually hold their wings out horizontally when they are not flying.

Though it is easy to tell damselflies from dragonflies, identifying different kinds within each group can be quite difficult. In some species, adult males and females are different colors. An individual's color can change over time as well. A breeding male may be much brighter than a young or aging one. Identifying nymphs can be even harder than identifying adults. In fact, many species of odonates are known only from adult specimens; scientists are not sure what the nymphs look like! Sometimes entomologists have to raise a nymph to adulthood in order to identify it.

Metamorphosis

An odonate nymph molts many times underwater. When it is ready for its final molt, it crawls up a plant stem, or rock, or onto shore until

its entire body is out of the water. Its skin splits, and the adult crawls out, unfolding a surprisingly long abdomen and wings. The newly emerged adult is called an **imago.** When its wings are dry and its body is hard, it will fly off in search of food.

Life in the air

Dragonflies and damselflies live just a few weeks as airborne adults. During this time you can watch them hunt, patrol their territories, court, mate, and lay eggs. Female odonates deposit their eggs in water. Some fly above the surface, dipping their abdomens down into the water and releasing eggs as they go. Others lay eggs on aquatic plants, or in the sand or mud near shore. Adult odonates have huge

eyes, which help them locate flying insects to eat. They snatch their prey out of the air with their long legs, which form a kind of basket when they fly.

Rearing damselflies and dragonflies

Nymphs from still water are easy to raise as long as you provide them with plenty of food! Keep them in aquaria or shallow pans with a layer of sand, gravel, or pond muck on the bottom. Replace evaporated water with pond or spring water rather than tap water, as the chemicals in tap water may harm aquatic animals. You can collect small crustacea and insects from a pond for them to eat. Lean a stick against the side of the container, or roll a strip of gauze or cheesecloth down into

the water so the nymphs can crawl out when it is time for their metamorphosis to adulthood.

Most odonate nymphs live underwater for about a year, though some damselfly species mature in just a few months. Large dragonflies may take three or four years.

21

Damselflies mating

Crickets

Katydid nymph.

With patience, you can learn a great deal about crickets by observing them outdoors. Many are **territorial**, so once you find a cricket, you may well be able to locate it again. Cricket territories are, by our standards, fairly small, so you can keep track of a cricket as it moves about within its territory.

It is also easy to keep crickets indoors, in order to make close observations over an extended period of time. Crickets will even mate and lay eggs in captivity if you feed and house them properly.

Finding crickets

In warm climates, you can find crickets throughout the year. In cooler climates, most adults die when frosty weather hits, leaving their eggs to overwinter in the ground. In the spring, these eggs hatch, and small cricket nymphs emerge. By midsummer, a series of molts will have transformed them into adults. You can find crickets by looking around stones and foundations, in buildings, gardens, vacant

lots, and fields. If you have trouble finding some, rake together a pile of grass clippings, hay, or weeds. If the weather is warm, crickets will come by the dozen. You can also listen for crickets. In late summer and fall, the chirping calls that

adult males make to attract mates draw our attention, too. If looking and listening don't bring you to crickets, you can purchase them. Bait shops and pet stores sell them, or you can order them from one of the biological supply houses mentioned on page 62.

Crickets are good jumpers, so they can be tricky to catch. If you are quick, you can scoop them up in your hands. A net or plastic container can help.

Raising crickets

There are more than one thousand species of crickets. Field crickets (*Gryllus sp.*) and house crickets (*Acheta domesticus*) are among the

most familiar. Both are in the family Gryllidae, and are easy to raise.

Housing: Glass or clear plastic containers will give you the best view of your crickets; large aquaria work particularly well. A tight-fitting top made from wire screening or cheesecloth will keep crickets inside. Get enough sand, soil, or peat moss to make a one- or two-inch layer on the bottom of your container. Bake the material at 200 degrees F for two hours to sterilize it. This will help prevent the growth of fungi. Place the soil in your container, mist it with water, and check it periodically. Some moisture will encourage females to lay eggs, and it may help

the eggs develop, but they won't hatch if the soil is really wet. Add a few stones, cardboard tubes, or other "hiding places."

Food: Crickets have strong chewing mouthparts. They can eat an enormous variety of things: plants, other insects, even cloth and leather! Dry dog food pellets are even a possibility for captive crickets. You can vary their diet with small slices of fruit and vegetables. Make sure that food is removed before it starts to rot.

Water: Crickets can get water by eating moist food or by drinking water sprinkled on rocks in the cage. Small bottles of water plugged with clean pieces of sponge, and jar lids containing wet pieces of sponge also work. Keep an eye on the amount of moisture in your tank. Crickets need moisture, but too much can cause problems.

Numbers: Male crickets often claim a particular territory, make sounds to warn others away, and chase or kick intruders. Too many crickets in one container will lead to aggression and injury. If your container is small (a one-gallon fish tank, for example), keep only one male and a female or two. Larger containers, well supplied with "hiding places" and things to crawl on, can hold more.

Observing crickets

Male and female crickets can be seen eating, drinking, and grooming. Crickets depend heavily on their antennae for important information about their surroundings. They keep their antennae clean by pulling them one at a time through their jaws. Males make sounds by rubbing a ridge on one wing across a scraper on the other,

so you can see, as well as hear, males chirp. You can also observe how females respond. Crickets have eardrums on their front legs, and though you cannot see them without magnification, it is fun to know how crickets are able to hear one another. You may see males and females mating, or females laying eggs. Females push their **ovipositors** into the soil to deposit their eggs.

Taxonomy

ORDER: **Orthoptera (grasshoppers, katydids, crickets, mantids, walkingsticks, and cockroaches)**
SUBORDER: **Ensifera (orthopterans with long, slender ovipositors and antennae, and eardrums on their front legs)**
FAMILY: **Gryllidae (crickets)**
SUBFAMILIES: **Gryllotalpinae (mole crickets), Eneopterinae and Trigonidiinae (bush crickets), Oecanthinae (tree crickets), Nemobiinae (ground crickets), Gryllinae (field and house crickets)**

Slim Chances

Though you may sometimes think that our planet is overrun with insects, a little math shows that the situation could be really drastic.

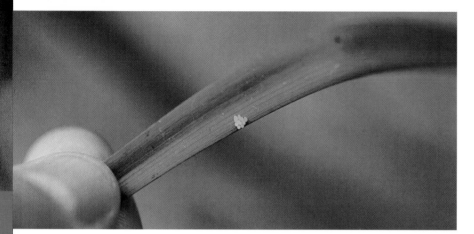

Reproductive potential

One praying mantis egg case may contain several hundred eggs, and a single female may make fifteen or more cases. Some mosquitoes can lay five hundred eggs at a time, and may mate and lay eggs several times in a row. One ladybug can lay as many as fifteen hundred eggs in her lifetime. Animals capable of producing large numbers of offspring in a short time are said to have a high **reproductive potential.**

Flooded with flies

Female houseflies can lay several hundred eggs at a time, and they lay a new batch every ten days. Since the eggs only take eight to twelve hours to hatch, and the larvae mature and are ready to mate themselves within two weeks, these insects are capable of reproducing at a truly staggering rate.

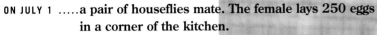

ON JULY 1 .....a pair of houseflies mate. The female lays 250 eggs in a corner of the kitchen.

ON JULY 2 .....the housefly population in the kitchen numbers 2 adults and 250 tiny, new larvae.

ON JULY 10 ....the original pair have mated again and produced 250 more eggs.

ON JULY 15 ....the population numbers 502: the 2 original adults, 250 new adults from the first batch of eggs, and 250 larvae from the second batch of eggs.

ON JULY 16 ....the new adults have mated. If half are females and each lays 250 eggs, the total number of new eggs is 31,250.

ON JULY 17 ....the count is 252 adults and 31,250 larvae. And in three days the original pair will be ready to mate again.

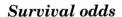

Survival odds

Many insect eggs never hatch. Unfavorable weather and climate conditions may kill them, or birds may find and eat them. Chances are, the nymphs and larvae that do hatch will not survive long enough to reproduce. Mammals as small as bats and as large as bears eat insects; so do fish, centipedes, spiders, and scores of other animals, including many species of insects. Diseases, parasites, and weather also take their toll. Though their reproductive potential is high, most insects' chances for survival are low.

WARNING PREDATORS

Many animals prey on insects. Over the past 250 million years, insects have evolved with special abilities to avoid becoming another animal's dinner.

Eating poison

Milkweed bugs eat milkweed seeds. These seeds, like the rest of the milk-weed plant, contain chemicals called **glycosides**. Glycosides are poisonous to many animals, but milkweed bugs aren't bothered by them. As the bugs eat, glycosides are concentrated in their bodies. Predators unfortunate enough to catch a milkweed bug may find it bad tasting, or even poisonous.

Advertising

Milkweed bugs, monarch butterflies, and many other milkweed-eaters are brightly colored. Instead of blending in with their surroundings, they show up easily. Scientists think these bright colors may advertise their toxicity, warning predators to stay away. Here's how it works: a predator, for example, a bird, catches a red-and-black, milkweed-eating insect. The bird might react to the glycoside taste and drop the insect instead of eating it. Or the bird might go ahead and eat the insect, getting sick as a result. In either case, the bird associates red-and-black insects with a bad experience, and avoids eating them in the future. Of course, no defense is perfect; just as a few species of insects have evolved an immunity to glycosides, a few predators have evolved an immunity to insects that concentrate glycosides.

A milkweed community

Field observations will help you learn about the insect communities associated with milkweed. How many different species of insects can be found on one plant? At what time of year does each make its appearance? What part of the plant does each species feed on?

Raising Milkweed Bugs

 Raising milkweed bugs will give you a chance to observe the life cycle of an insect with gradual metamorphosis. Milkweed bugs belong to the family Lygeidae, or seed bugs.

Finding milkweed bugs

If you live in an area where milkweed plants are common, you will probably be able to find milkweed bugs. The large milkweed bug, *Oncopeltus fasciatus*, reaches a length of about one-half inch. You may also find the small milkweed bug, *Lygaeus kalmii*. Milkweed

bugs thrive in warm weather, and in some places you can find adults year round. In northern areas many nymphs and adults die when cold weather hits, and some adults migrate south. Although a new generation will return north the following summer, you may not start finding them until mid-season.

You can find adults and nymphs crawling among milkweed flowers and on the underside of leaves. You may also find them on the ground at the base of the milkweed plant, for if they were disturbed by your approach, they may drop to the ground to keep out of harm's way. You may even find milkweed bug eggs, which are laid in clusters of fifteen to thirty under leaves or between pods.

Look through a hand lens to get a close-up view of milkweed bugs.

Mail order bugs

If you live in an area where milkweed is not common, or if you want to raise milkweed bugs at a time of year when they cannot be found outdoors, you can order some from a biological supply company (see page 62). Supply companies collect or raise organisms that interest students and researchers, and for a few dollars you can have milkweed bugs delivered to your door. Milkweed bugs obtained from a supply house are easier to maintain than wild ones, for they have been bred to feed on sunflower seeds instead of milkweed pods.

REMEMBER: If you live in an area where milkweed bugs are not native, you will need to freeze any insects and eggs that are alive when you have finished studying them. Releasing insects outdoors in an area where they do not ordinarily live can cause trouble. They might fail to find food and starve to death. Or more problematically, they might thrive and reproduce overwhelmingly, unchecked by native predators.

Housing and feeding your bugs

Keep your milkweed bugs in a clean, dry container. A one-gallon glass jar, a small aquarium, or a cage made with wire screening will do. Wild bugs need to be supplied with milkweed pods containing seeds. Nymphs will feed on flowers as well. Mail order bugs can be given hulled, unsalted sunflower seeds. A small vial of water plugged with cotton or a piece of damp sponge will provide enough water for your bugs. Of course, your container will need a bug-proof lid. Cheesecloth and screening both work well. Make

8

Place a cotton ball or piece of cloth inside a small jar, lid, or cup and put it in your container. This will make a milkweed leaf substitute for the females to lay eggs on. If your container becomes crowded with bugs, move the eggs to a new jar. A single female may lay as many as two thousand eggs in her lifetime, and overcrowding can lead to cannibalism.

They will molt five times before they are fully grown. The stage between each molt is called an instar. Observing the shed exoskeletons as well as the actual nymphs will help you to understand what changes occur between instars.

sure that fresh food and water are always available. Since bugs feed by sucking the contents of a seed and leaving the outside, you will need to remove the shrunken seed casings that are left behind.

What can you notice?

Adult milkweed bugs live for thirty to forty days. During that time they mate, and females lay eggs. You can tell adult males from females by the color pattern on the **ventral**, or under, side of their abdomens.

Eggs hatch in about four days. Newly hatched nymphs are tiny— as small as the head of a pin!

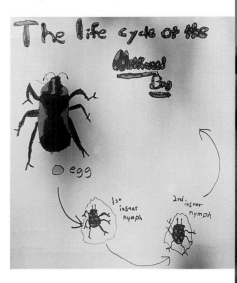

Males have two black bands separated by a plain band of orange. In females, the orange band has a black spot on each side.

Taxonomy

ORDER: *Hemiptera (bugs)*
FAMILY: *Lygeidae (seed bugs)*
GENUS AND SPECIES: *Oncopeltus fasciatus (the large milkweed bug), Lygaeus kalmii (the small milkweed bug)*

INSECTS AND PLANTS

The lives of insects and plants are interestingly intertwined. Many insects depend on certain kinds of plants for food or shelter.

Picky eaters

Grape leaf skeletonizers are the larvae of *Harrisina americana*, the grape leaf skeletonizer moth. They feed in groups, chewing their way across the leaves of grapes, Virginia creepers, redbuds or ampelopsis. Just as some people eat bread but leave the crusts, grape leaf skeletonizers eat leaves but forsake the stem and veins.

Garden gourmets

The asparagus beetle, *Crioceris asparagi*, and the spotted asparagus beetle, *Crioceris duodecimpunctata*, both dine on asparagus. Unlike human gourmets, they focus on the delicate leaves as well as the tender young shoots. Adult asparagus beetles are small, only about a quarter-inch in length. They spend the winter in weeds or mulch near asparagus beds. In the spring, adults mate and lay rows of tiny eggs on young asparagus spears. The eggs hatch into tiny beetle larvae. They are hard to spot, as their coloring camouflages them against asparagus foliage. Asparagus beetles belong to a group known as the shining leaf beetles, in the family Chrysomelidae.

Leaf folders and rollers

You may have seen a plant with leaves that looked strange, as though someone or something had folded them over, rolled

Taxonomy

ORDER:
    Lepidoptera (moths and butterflies)
FAMILY: *Zygaenidae (smoky moths)*
GENUS AND SPECIES:
    Harrisina americana (the grape leaf skeletonizer)

Taxonomy

ORDER: *Coleoptera (beetles)*
FAMILY: *Chrysomelidae (leaf beetles)*
GENUS AND SPECIES:
    Crioceris asparagi (the asparagus beetle), Crioceris duodecimpunctata (the spotted asparagus beetle)

them up, or stuck them to other leaves. Most likely it was a caterpillar.

Many species of caterpillars roll, fold, or "tie" leaves, fastening them together with silk thread that comes out of a gland in their mouths. The leaves provide food, and the folds offer protection from predators, and from weather as well. Different species of caterpillars have characteristic ways of shaping leaves, and many are particular about the kinds of leaves they will use. Some newly hatched caterpillars make a small fold along one edge of a leaf. They chew on the part that curves to the inside. As they eat, they grow and molt. They enlarge their homes by rolling over a little more of the leaf and securing it with silk. This turns a little more of the leaf to the inside, where it stops providing shelter and starts providing food. Some caterpillars begin by shaping one leaf, and then fasten together several more later on.

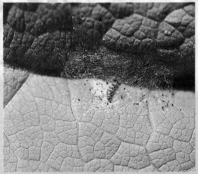

Leaf rolls like these may house a moth caterpillar or cocoon.

A partially skeletonized oak leaf.

Galls

Galls are abnormal growths on plants. They are evidence of another fascinating relationship between insects and plants. Many kinds of galls are caused (or **induced**) by insects. A gall is formed when a female insect lays an egg on or in a plant. She may also deposit a chemical on the plant. This chemical, or the secretions or feeding activity of the newly hatched larva, makes the plant grow in an unusual way. The swelling plant tissue surrounds the developing larva, providing it with food and shelter.

How to find galls

You can hunt for galls wherever there are plants. Look for unusual spots or swellings on leaves, twigs, and stems. Goldenrod flowers and oak trees are especially good plants to search because they tend to have more galls than many other species. Scientists aren't sure why.

Once you start looking for galls, you will discover many different kinds. Gall-inducing insects are particular about the plants they lay their eggs on, and each species of insect causes a specific type of gall.

Noting what the gall looks like and identifying the plant it is on will help you determine what kind of insect induced it, even if the insect itself has matured and left.

Goldenrod galls

Goldenrod ball galls are induced by *Eurosta solidaginis*, a fruit fly.

Fly larvae spend the winter inside ball galls, then pupate and emerge as adults in the spring. Elliptical goldenrod galls have small caterpillars inside. Eventually, they emerge as moths. Blister galls look like black spots on goldenrod leaves. They are caused by a type of midge (an insect in the order Diptera).

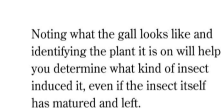

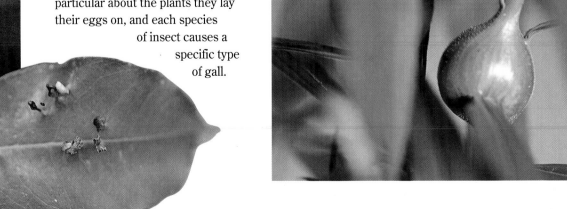

Oak apples

Hundreds of different kinds of galls can be found on oak trees. Oak apple galls, which grow on twigs and leaves, are some of the more obvious. They are light brown or tan, and can be an inch or two in diameter. Tiny wasp larvae live at the center, surrounded by hair-like fibers that radiate outward. There are many kinds of oak apples, each caused by a different species of wasp in the family Cynipidae.

Common and confounding

Galls are common, but entomologists still have a lot to learn about the insects that cause them. Most gall makers are tiny. As larvae they are hidden inside plants, and as adults they can be hard to find. This makes them both fascinating and difficult to study! There are about fifteen hundred species of insects in North America that induce galls. Certain mites, nematode worms, bacteria, and fungi can induce galls as well.

Anybody home?

If you carefully search the surface of a gall, you may find tiny **exit holes** where the inhabitant chewed its way out of its former home. Large holes in the gall are apt to be the work of another animal; downy woodpeckers, red squirrels, and certain species of mice have learned to search out galls in order to eat the larvae inside. Small spiders and insects may move into a gall if the original inhabitant gets eaten or moves on.

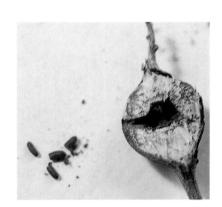

Galls without exit holes may still harbor the inducing insect, but sometimes they hold surprises. New insects may move in alongside the original larvae, or parasitic insects may lay their eggs within the gall. When parasite larvae hatch, they feed upon the gall maker.

Gall-Watching

If you want to see what emerges from a gall, you can dig up the entire plant it is on and pot it indoors. You can also leave the gall where you find it, but cover it with a bag sewn of flexible tent screening so the emerging insect can't fly away until you've had a look at it. Some host plants die or enter a **dormant** period in the fall. When they do, you can collect some of their galls and keep them indoors in a shoebox or empty jar until the insects inside tunnel out. Be prepared to be patient! Some larvae eat and grow inside a gall all summer, pupate over the winter, and emerge as adults the following spring.

STAYING SAFE

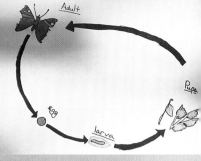

Insects have developed a variety of ways to protect themselves. Some insects are brightly colored, warning predators of their bitter taste, and others hide out in galls. There are other ways that insects stay safe, too.

Blending in

Katydids spend most of their time in trees, which is why people seldom see them. Plenty of other animals spend time in trees, too, and many of them eat insects! How can a katydid avoid predators? Protective coloration may help. Katydids are bright green, so even though they are large, they blend in well with the leaves they walk on and eat. Many other plant-eating insects are green, too.

You may have heard katydids on summer and early autumn nights. The males make loud sounds by rubbing their forewings together. Females are attracted by the sounds. Katydids, like crickets and grasshoppers, are members of the order Orthoptera.

Taxonomy

ORDER: **Orthoptera**
SUBORDER: **Ensifera**
FAMILY: **Tettigoniidae**
    (the "long-horned
    grasshoppers")
SUBFAMILY:
    Phaneropterinae
    (bush and round-headed
    katydids)

Life among nettles

Stinging nettles, *Urtica dioica*, are common in fields, vacant lots, and along roadsides. They are plants to look out for! They look harmless, but are covered with tiny hairs filled with formic acid. If you accidentally touch a nettle, the acid will sting your skin. This sting may offer nettles some protection from plant-eating animals.

One animal actually seeks out stinging nettles. The red admiral butterfly, *Vanessa atalanta*, lays her eggs on them. When the eggs hatch, the larvae feed on the leaves. A larva can pull the sides of a leaf together by fastening them with silk. The folded leaf, covered with acid-filled hairs, makes a safe place for the larva to pupate.

Taxonomy

ORDER: **Lepidoptera**
FAMILY: **Nymphalidae**
    (brush-footed butterflies)
GENUS AND SPECIES:
    Vanessa atalanta
    (red admiral butterfly)

Mimicry

Will the real bumblebee please stand up?

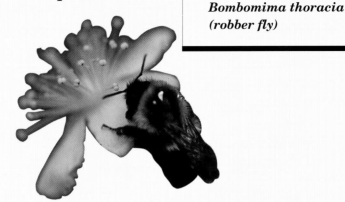

Taxonomy

ORDER: *Diptera*
FAMILY: *Asilidae*
GENUS AND SPECIES:
Bombomima thoracia
(robber fly)

Both of these insects look like bees, but one of them is an impostor. What's going on? The insect on the left is a bee-mimicking fly. It belongs to a group of insects known as robber flies, and like other mimics, it bears a superficial resemblance to another species. This may be useful when it comes to escaping predators. Bumblebees can sting when threatened. Robber flies are not so well equipped. Predators, however, may not be able to distinguish the two species, and will avoid the fly as well as the bee.

Passing as a bee may also help the fly find food. Bumblebees feed on nectar. Other insects foraging in the vicinity of a bumblebee are apt not to be disturbed, as the bee poses no threat to them. But robber flies hunt other insects. A fly in bee's clothing may stand a better chance of sneaking up on its prey than one that is clearly recognizable as a predator.

Of course, the robber fly is not involved in a deliberate hoax. Genetics, not intentions, determine its appearance. Biologists think that one species may evolve to resemble another. In each generation, the individuals best suited to the conditions they find themselves in are most likely to live long enough to reproduce. Variations in appearance or behavior give individuals unequal chances for survival. Ancestral robber flies may have looked quite different than bees. Over many generations, however, some traits may have died out while others developed, so today the two insects look similar.

BEES BELONG TO THE ORDER HYMENOPTERA.

Bees have:
- relatively long antennae
- moderately large compound eyes
- four wings
- chewing mouthparts
- stingers

FLIES BELONG TO THE ORDER DIPTERA.

Flies have:
- short, inconspicuous antennae
- very large compound eyes
- two wings
- sucking mouthparts

Pollinators

I n order for flowering plants to produce fruit and seeds, they must be **pollinated**. That means tiny grains of pollen must be moved from one part of a flower (the **anther**) to another part (the **stigma**). In most species, pollen must move from one flower to another as well (**cross-pollination**). Some plants are pollinated when the wind blows. Water and birds can carry pollen, too. Insects do most of the pollinating on the planet, though; more than two-thirds of all flowering plants depend on them.

Busy bees

You may have seen a bumblebee visiting a flower. Bumblebees actually collect pollen from flowers; they use it to feed their young. Hairs on their hind legs hold the pollen, and they use their front legs to gather it and to pack it into their **pollen baskets**. A bumblebee will stop at a number of flowers before returning to her underground nest to "unload." Pollination occurs when some of the pollen grains she collects at one flower brush off on the next flower she visits.

Bumblebees collect nectar, too. **Nectar** is a sugary liquid produced by many insect-pollinated plants. It is food for adult bumblebees. Scientists think that flowering plants and insects have changed together, or co-evolved, over millions of years. Many species now depend on each other quite completely.

Bumblebees (and many other insects) rely on flowers for food. Flowers, in turn, require insect pollinators, and their nectar attracts insects to them. Some flowering plants that are pollinated by bumblebees or other insects are: goldenrod, st. johnswort, apple trees, and sunflowers.

Bees use their long tongues to get nectar from flowers.

Marking Bees

This bee is being marked with a small dot of typewriter correction fluid. Small dots are used so the fluid doesn't cover the bee's **spiracles**, or breathing holes, and keep it from getting air. The bee, in-

tent on getting nectar, is undisturbed.

Researchers trying to learn about an animal's behavior need to be able to tell it apart from other, similar looking, animals. Individual bees of the same species look so much alike that it is usually impossible to tell if the one you see on a particular flower in the morning is the same one you see there in the afternoon. Entomologists have developed ways of distinguishing individual insects and groups of insects by coding the insects' bodies with different colors or other identifying marks. These techniques have

enabled researchers to learn about migratory routes, population sizes, and the distances that insects travel in search of food.

HONEYBEES

H oneybees (*Apis mellifera*) are social insects. That means they live together in groups, or colonies, with each individual working to help the whole group survive.

Apis mellifera is one of the few domestic insects. Most of them live in hives constructed by people. Scientists think honeybees originated in Africa and were brought to many other parts of the world because people find them so useful. They are important pollinators of flowering plants, including apple trees and many others we raise for food, and they make wax and honey.

Queens, drones, and workers

Three castes, or groups, of honeybees live in a hive. These castes look different from one another, and each has particular work to do. The queen is the largest bee in the colony. She spends her time inside the hive, laying eggs. Drones, the males, mate with the queen. Workers are genetic females, but they are unable to reproduce. Young workers tend to the "housework;" they clean and maintain the hive, and feed the queen and larvae. Older workers gather pollen and nectar. Honeybees are quite efficient about gathering food. Once a worker finds pollen and nectar in a particular area, she will make repeated trips to that area to collect more and more. If there are several kinds of flowers blooming in the same area, she will focus on just one. Keying into a particular flower and location saves search time. When the worker has exhausted one food supply, she goes exploring to find others.

A worker can also help her sisters to find food. When she enters the hive with a load of nectar and pollen, she begins a special dance. Her dance lets other workers know exactly where to find the flowers she has just visited. Her movements show what direction they will need to fly in when they leave the hive, and how far to go. The smell of the nectar on the worker's body tells her partners what kind of flower to look for.

Taxonomy

ORDER: *Hymenoptera*
    (bees, wasps, and ants)
FAMILY: *Apidae*
GENUS AND SPECIES:
    Apis mellifera
    (honeybee)

Making honey

Bees change nectar into honey. Workers carry nectar to the hive in their crop, a storage chamber for swallowed food. Inside the hive, they give the nectar to other workers by regurgitating it. The hive workers mix it with a special chemical and some air in their mouths. This changes the nectar into honey, which is stored in wax cells and used later for food.

Keeping bees

Beekeepers set up wooden hives for their bees to live in. Frames inside the hive provide places for the bees to build the wax cells, or honeycomb, that house their young and serve as a storage place for honey. Beekeepers can buy bees, or capture a swarm. A swarm is a group of workers and a queen that have left their hive in search of a new place to live. Swarming bees are usually gentle and easy for a beekeeper to handle.

Beekeepers leave some honey in the hive to provide food for the bees, but they also remove honey to eat or sell. Smoking the hive calms the bees, and makes it safer for the beekeeper to remove honey-filled combs.

Beekeepers may sell the combs, or beeswax, as well as the honey. They also rent hives of bees to fruit growers when trees are in bloom and need to be pollinated.

39

Under the Eaves

We live in buildings. Some insects live on buildings.

Polistes wasps

This nest is made of paper. It was made by a polistes wasp. During the summer it is the site of much activity, but in late fall it is empty. The queen that made it and most of her offspring are dead, victims of cold weather and old age. But a new generation of queens, who flew from the nest and mated at the end of the summer, are hidden away in cracks and crevasses, waiting out the winter months in a state called **diapause.**

In spring, these new queens are ready to lay eggs. They return to the area where they were hatched to choose a nest site. A number of queens produced by the same nest may compete for sites, and sometimes a small group bands together to work. In this case, a **hierarchy** is established, with one queen laying eggs and the others building and caring for the young. During the spring and early summer, there

may be quite a bit of social reorganization. A solitary queen may abandon her nest and join a group of sisters. A queen may leave her nest or die, and a sister will replace her as the dominant, reproductive female.

To make their nests, polistes wasps scrape fibers from plant stems, weathered boards, and dead trees. They gather the fibers with their strong mouthparts, then chew them, mixing in saliva. Eventually this forms a pulpy building material. When dry, it feels like paper. Mouthful by mouthful, polistes queens attach a stalk to some surface, then add a tier of cells. You will often find their nests under the eaves of houses or attached to the ceilings of porches and outbuildings. Since they do not add an out

side covering as some species do, you can get good views of their activities.

Polistes wasps are less easily provoked to sting than yellow jackets or hornets, so observing them at work is relatively safe. Move slowly and keep your distance to avoid threatening them, and be alert for changes in behavior that may indicate they are becoming annoyed.

A polistes queen lays an egg in each cell of her nest. The eggs hatch into larvae that remain in the cells. The queen hunts for insects, particularly caterpillars, which she chews up and feeds to the larvae. Eventually the larvae pupate in their cells, emerging as adults. In the spring and early summer, only female workers emerge. They help

A wasp gathers material for a nest.

Taxonomy

ORDER: *Hymenoptera
(ants, bees, and wasps)*
FAMILIES: *Vespidae
Sphecidae*
SUBFAMILIES: *Eumeninae
(potter wasps),
Trypoxyloninae (organ
pipe mud daubers),
Polistinae
(paper wasps)*

the queen care for the larvae and work on the nest, but they do not lay eggs. The workers collect nectar which they eat themselves, and they gather and chew caterpillars to feed the larvae. The larvae, in turn, contribute to the adults' welfare by producing a kind of sweet saliva which the adults eat.

At the end of the summer, the nest produces larger females and males. They leave the nest and mate, and the new queens search out safe places to spend the winter.

Wasps in the genus Polistes belong to the family Vespidae. Like other members of this family, they are sometimes called paper wasps. Polistes wasps are brown, or brown and yellow, with long legs.

Diggers, daubers, and potters

Some wasps make special cases out of mud. These cases protect their eggs and developing young. Females of different species construct characteristic cases in the ground or in plant stems, or attach them to vegetation or buildings.

Mud daubers and potter wasps are **solitary insects.** A female will not stay with her eggs until they hatch, or even care for the larvae. Instead, she lays an egg inside the mud case (or in each cell of a case with multiple compartments), stuffs a caterpillar inside, and seals it with additional mud. When the egg hatches, the growing larva feeds on the caterpillar. The larva pupates inside the case and soon emerges as an adult. Digging wasps provide for their young in a similar way by

leaving a dead insect near each egg. They lay their eggs underground in holes they dig with their feet.

Look for wasp constructions on twigs and walls of buildings. You may even see wasps collecting mud near puddles or in damp garden soil. Some vespid wasps, and members of a few other families as well, build structures with mud.

EXPLORING THE

You don't have to go far to find interesting insects to study. You don't even have to set foot outdoors. House crickets, fruit flies, cockroaches, and clothes moths often share people's homes. So do fleas, flies, and carpenter ants. Some insects, like mosquitoes, are just passing through. Others, like termites, usually move in for good. Go inside and take a good look around. What insects live with you?

Flies, carpenter ants, and termites are insects you might find sharing your home.

Cockroaches

©BILL IVY

There are thousands of species of cockroaches in the world. If you live in a city, chances are you will be able to find *Blatella germanica,* the German cockroach, without looking hard at all. These insects live in all kinds of buildings: apartments, stores, schools, subway stations, museums, and restaurants. Domestic cockroaches are perfectly adapted for life among people. Their flattened bodies fit easily into tiny cracks in walls or spaces under objects. They are fast runners, with nervous systems that enable them to get moving almost as soon as they perceive danger. Long, sensitive antennae and cerci collect information about their surroundings, helping them to find food and water, and avoid danger. Finding food is rarely a problem. *B. germanica* can eat any food crumbs or scraps of food we happen to leave out for them.

If we clean up carefully after every meal, they can make do with cat food left out in a dish, insulation, the glue on wallpaper, stamps, and bookbindings, whatever is handy. They can even do without food and water for weeks at a time. As insects go, domestic cockroaches appear to be fairly intelligent. In laboratories, they have learned to run mazes and avoid areas sprayed with particular insecticides.

Other cockroaches, like the woodroach, are usually found outside. Outdoor roaches tend to spend their days in moist places: under stones, plants, logs, or among fallen leaves. Like indoor roaches, they are most active at night, and find places to hide during the day. Water pipes, kitchens, bathrooms, and other damp places often attract indoor roaches. Cockroaches are ancient animals. Fossils as old as 250 million years have been found that look quite similar to today's species. Apparently, cockroaches were as well suited to life among dinosaurs as they are to life among people.

GREAT INDOORS

Window lights and street lights

Some insects are attracted to light, and will fly to lighted windows at night. You can easily observe them from inside, or you can take a flashlight and go out. You may discover many species that are new to you crawling across your screens on a summer evening. Check porch lights and streetlamps, too. Moths, beetles, and other insects are often drawn to them. Insects that have accidentally ended up inside a building may fly at windows during the day in search of a way back out.

Making a Collection

Making a collection can help you learn more about insect anatomy, identification, and classification. You may want to collect a variety of insects, or just one species.

Equipment

Before you start collecting insects, assemble the following equipment. It will help you with your work.

A **net** can help you catch insects that are difficult to capture with your bare hands.

A **killing can** is used to contain and kill insects. Coffee cans with plastic lids work well.

Pins are used to mount many insects. Use special insect pins rather than sewing pins, which may rust or be too thick for some delicate insects. Pins come in many sizes: 0, 1, 2, and 3 will be most useful. You can order them from one of the supply houses listed on page 62.

Boxes with cork or foam lining the bottom are used to mount and store specimens. You can adapt a cigar box, but boxes specifically designed for collectors are easiest to use. They are available from biological supply houses.

How to kill insects

Some entomologists use poisons to kill insects, but a much safer method also works. Simply leave the insects in a covered can and put the can in a freezer for a few hours. Once the insects are dead, let them thaw out before you handle them.

Conservation

Be selective when you collect. Here are some guidelines:
▶ Collect only one specimen of any species, unless it is considered a **pest**.
▶ Collect all the pests you want, such as Japanese beetles, gypsy moths, and cabbage-white butterflies.
▶ Collect only adult insects. Leave larvae and nymphs. Most larvae and nymphs require special preservation techniques.
▶ Collect insects that are already dead.
▶ Release insects that help control pests, such as praying mantids and ladybeetles.
▶ Release insects that are rare, or uncommon to your particular collecting site.

This Japanese beetle is considered a pest; collect as many as you want.

Collecting

You can pick insects up with your fingers, or catch them with a net. To transfer them to your killing can, hold the tip of your net straight up so that the insects will work their way up into it. Then gently invert the end of the net into your open can. It takes practice to learn to do this successfully; you may lose some insects in the beginning. Observe and then release insects that you do not plan to add to your collection.

Field notes

Make sure to record the date and location where you collect a specimen. You can also make field notes about its behavior or appearance.

Pinning

Many insects can be pinned directly into storage and display boxes.

Choose the pin size that is appropriate for each specimen. Beetles and leafhoppers are usually pinned through the right wing, bugs are pinned above the "X" formed by the crossed forewings, and flies and grasshoppers are pinned through the right part of the thorax. Some insects are so small that even the finest of pins are too large for them. These insects can be fixed to a small triangle of stiff paper with a dot of glue. The pin can be put through the paper instead of directly through the insect. Make sure to pin insects soon after they are killed so that they don't become brittle. You can keep them in an airtight

box in the freezer if there will be several days between collecting and pinning. If specimens become too brittle to work with, they can be relaxed by putting them in a jar with a damp piece of blotting paper or a few drops of water on the bottom.

Spreading

Butterflies, dragonflies, grasshoppers, and many other insects are often displayed with one or both pairs of wings open. **Spreading boards** are used to prepare these specimens. First, position the insect with its body in the center groove of the spreading board. Pin strips of paper over the wings. Remove one pin and gently position the wing nearest it with a tweezers. Replace the pin, and continue until all wings are positioned. Leave the insect on the board until it is completely dry. This may take a few days or as long as two weeks.

Labeling

Two labels made of heavy paper are usually pinned underneath each insect in a collection. The first identifies the insect and lists the date and place it was captured. The collector's name is put on a second label.

Protecting your collection

Store your collection in a dry place. Make sure that the box lid fits tightly. Dermestid beetles will eat dried insects, among other things, and a tight lid will discourage them from making a meal of your collection. Some collectors add mothballs or flakes to their boxes to keep dermestids away.

Identifying Insects

I dentifying insects means recognizing the details of behavior or appearance that distinguish one type of insect from another. Identification can occur at many levels. Sometimes you simply want to know if the animal you are observing is an insect or another kind of arthropod.

Is it a beetle or a bug?

Often, you know you have found an insect but aren't sure whether to call it a beetle or a bug. With experience you will be able to identify most insects you find to the level of order. That is, you will be able to tell a beetle (Coleoptera) from a bug (Hemiptera), and a bug (Hemiptera) from an aphid (Homoptera). Sometimes it is important to be able to identify an insect more exactly, but often, figuring out what order an insect belongs to will be enough to help you make sense of your observations and find reference materials to further your work.

Field guides

Field guides are books designed to help people recognize the plants, animals, and minerals that surround us. Many have been written about insects. They have drawings or photographs of insects that you can compare to the actual animal you are looking at, and written descriptions to check. Look for a field guide to the insects native to your area at your local library or bookstore.

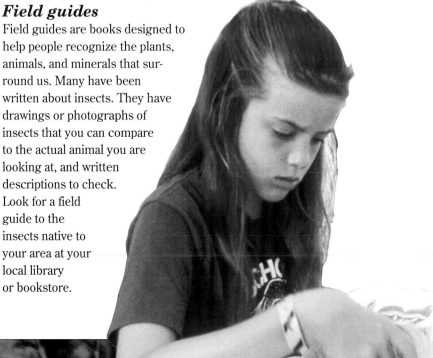

But what kind of beetle is it?

If you find an insect and want to figure out exactly what kind it is, you may have quite a challenge ahead of you. For one thing, there are so many species of insects that it is impossible to become familiar with all—or even most—of them. For another, sometimes different species resemble one another quite closely. Many insects are small, and you

may need a hand lens or microscope to find the tiny anatomical features that distinguish them. To complicate matters further, some insects go through dramatic changes during their lives. An insect may look entirely different as a larva than it does as an adult. A male may be different colors than a female of the same species. It takes experience and careful study to make accurate identifications, so call on a local county agent, teacher, naturalist, museum curator, or professional entomologist if you get stuck.

Fortunately, identifying insects is not always difficult. In some cases it is easy to know a species because of distinguishing characteristics that are easy to see. For example, the red bands and spots on the wings of the cecropia moth, *Hyalophora cecropia,* set it apart from the polyphemus moth, *Antheraea polyphemus*, a similar looking species in the same family. Sometimes behavior is a clue to a species identification; a white butterfly flitting around the broccoli or cabbage plants in a garden is bound to be *Pieris rapae*, the cabbage butterfly.

Microscopes

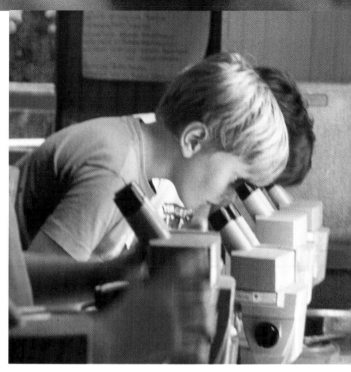

To see the thorns on a dragonfly's wing or the hundreds of facets in a housefly's compound eye, you'll need special equipment. Microscopes can help you observe these fascinating features, and make other amazing discoveries about familiar insects. Microscopes are also important tools when it comes to identifying insects. One family or genus may be distinguished from another by the number of segments on the insect's antennae or legs. Often these features are not visible without magnification.

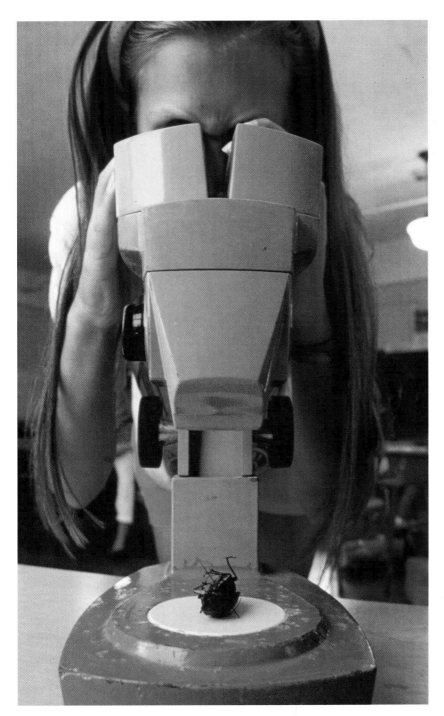

Inexpensive hand lenses and magnifiers with battery-run light bulbs also allow a closer look at insects.

Practicing

Using a hand lens, stereo microscope, or some other kind of magnifier takes some getting used to. Practice adjusting the focus. Experiment to find out how much light and what kind of background help you see each insect most clearly. Try to relate the enlarged image you see under magnification to the insect seen with your unaided eyes.

Different kinds of microscopes

There are different kinds of microscopes. Each has particular capabilities and is useful for certain types of research. A stereo microscope (also called a dissecting microscope) will help you study insects. Stereo microscopes are expensive, but schools often provide them for students to use. Both eyepieces are looked through at the same time, allowing some depth of field.

Magnification up to thirty times is possible. An entire insect can be placed on the stage of this kind of microscope, so you can use it to view living as well as preserved specimens.

Beetles

adybugs aren't actually bugs. They're beetles. Like all adult Coleoptera, they have a shiny, hard pair of wings, called elytra, covering their backs, with another pair of wings folded up underneath. When a ladybug flies, it holds its elytra out to its sides and beats its membranous flying wings. When it is not flying, the elytra meet together, forming a straight line down its back.

The ladybug lifecycle

Ladybugs undergo complete metamorphosis, as do all beetles. Adults mate, and the females lay clusters of tiny, yellow eggs on leaves. The eggs hatch within a week, and the larvae begin looking for aphids or other soft-bodied insects to eat.

Young beetles, or larvae, look

quite different from adults. Many have soft bodies that might remind you of caterpillars or worms, and shiny, hard heads with chewing mouthparts. Some species tunnel through the ground or under tree

bark, some live underwater, and others crawl around on plant leaves and stems.

During their pupal stage, beetles are basically inactive, though they may wiggle slightly if disturbed. Internally, their bodies are changing in form. When they emerge from

their pupal skins, their wings are fully developed. The hard elytra often cover up the entire abdomen.

Ladybugs, or more accurately lady beetles, often live for two or three years. In the fall, adults look

for a safe place to spend the winter. They may crawl under fallen leaves or the loose bark on a log. Some make their way into buildings instead, so keep an eye out for them at home and at school.

So far, Coleoptera is the largest order of insects, including nearly 300,000 species.

Japanese beetles

Japanese beetles, like honeybees, cabbage butterflies, and gypsy moths, have been transplanted by people to many parts of the globe. Native to Japan, *Popillia japonica* were discovered in New Jersey in 1916. Japanese beetle larvae live underground, and they were accidentally imported, hidden among the roots of plants. They are now common throughout much of the northeastern United States.

Japanese beetles are considered pests by many farmers and gardeners in the United States. The adults eat the leaves, flowers, and fruits of hundreds of species of plants, and the larvae feed on the roots. Though common enough in Japan, *P. japonica* do not cause the extensive damage there that they do in the United States. This is often the case with **introduced species.** In an animal's native environment, predators, diseases, or limited food supplies keep its numbers in check. But when an animal is suddenly introduced to a new area, it may be relatively free from these pressures, at least for a while. In its new home, population growth and range expansion can be rapid.

Human beings, deliberately and accidentally, alter the places where we live. Sometimes, as in the introduction of the honeybee and praying mantis, we profit. Other times, as in the case of the Japanese beetle or gypsy moth, we create a pest.

Rhinos and unicorns

The subfamily Dynastinae contains some very large beetles, including the unicorn, elephant, and rhinoceros beetles. Some species have bumps or horns on their heads.

Taxonomy

ORDER: *Coleoptera*
SUPERFAMILY: *Scarabaeoidea (terminal segments of antennae expanded sideways)*
FAMILY: *Scarabaeidae (scarab beetles)*
SUBFAMILY: *Rutelinae (shining leaf chafers) - adults eat leaves, flowers, and fruit, larvae feed on roots; tarsal claws of unequal length*
GENUS AND SPECIES: *Popillia japonica (Japanese beetle)*

51

Taxonomy

ORDER: *Coleoptera*
SUBFAMILY: *Dynastinae*
GENUS AND SPECIES: *Xylorcytes jamaicensis (rhinoceros beetle)*

This rhinoceros beetle is a male; females have much smaller horns.

FIELD TRIP APHIDS

These tiny, yellow insects are aphids. They are sucking juice out of a milkweed leaf. The chances are good that they were born on this leaf, and that they will remain on it for their entire lives. The largest aphids are adults, and the smaller ones are their daughters.

An unusual life cycle

Many species of aphids feed on a particular kind of plant, and most have unusual life cycles. In midsummer or fall, males and females mate. The females lay eggs on or near a food plant. The eggs remain dormant through the winter, and tiny, wingless females emerge in the spring. No males emerge at all, but the females, once mature, are still able to produce young. Instead of hatching from eggs, these young are born alive. They stay on the same plant as their mothers, feeding and growing. As adults, they give birth to more wingless females.

Eventually a generation is born that develops wings and flies off in search of new food plants. Once they locate the right kind of plant, these winged females give birth to wingless females, starting a new colony. Reproduction without fertilization is called **parthenogenesis**.

If you look closely you will see winged females who will give birth to wingless females through parthenogenesis.

As summer advances, the plants that aphids feed on stop growing and begin to dry out. Feeding becomes difficult. At this point adults give birth to both males and females. These mate, and the females lay fertilized eggs that overwinter. Tree-dwelling aphids may **aestivate**, or enter a dormant period, in late summer, becoming active for a while when tree growth resumes in the fall. But eventually, like the flower-dwellers, they are left without food.

Taxonomy

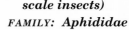

ORDER: **Homoptera (cicadas, hoppers, whiteflies, aphids, and scale insects)**
FAMILY: **Aphididae**

Finding aphids

Fields and gardens are good places to look for aphids. Check the leaves nearest the tips of plant stems. Sometimes you will find colonies of one hundred or more feeding together! When aphids become really plentiful on a plant, they may actually suck out so much juice that the leaves shrivel and turn brown. If you want to watch a colony over a period of time, you can dig up the plant they are on, or keep a few stems indoors in water. Aphids are tiny, so a hand lens might help you get a better look at them. Adults may not even reach a length of one-eighth of an inch.

Aphids and ants

Sometimes you will find a colony of aphids with some ants wandering among them. The ants are not hurting the aphids; in fact, they protect the aphids from predators like ladybugs and lacewing larvae. The ants are eating, feeding on a sweet liquid called **honeydew** that the aphids excrete. Aphids eliminate honeydew in order to get rid of the excess liquid that builds up in their bodies as a result of their watery diet. Many kinds of ants have learned to feed on honeydew, and can even get aphids to excrete it by stroking their bodies.

Some species of ants take particularly good care of their aphid "cows." In addition to defending aphids from predators during the day, they will bring them into the ant nest at night. Some ants collect aphid eggs in the fall and store them in their nests all winter. In the spring, they return them to the proper food plant. Because both the ants and aphids benefit from this relationship, entomologists refer to it as **mutualism**.

Parasites

Parasites are organisms that live on or in other **host** organisms. Though parasites benefit from this relationship, their hosts do not. Over time, parasites may irritate, weaken, or even kill their hosts.

Parasites of people

Head lice are insect parasites common to humans. Like it or not, our heads provide them with food, shelter, and transportation to new habitats. *Pediculus humanus* can live only a short time away from a human head, but once comfortably settled there, it goes about its business of finding food, mating, and laying eggs. Lice feed by biting their hosts on the scalp and withdrawing blood with their short, beak-like mouthparts. Eggs are attached singly to strands of hair. These "nits" are small, oblong, and immovable. An itchy scalp may be one sign of head lice. Nits are another. Nits hatch into nymphs, which grow into adults through gradual metamorphosis. Special combs and chemical shampoos are used to get rid of lice.

54

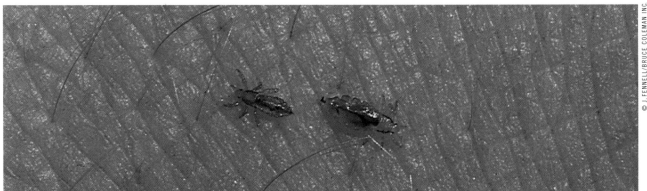

Taxonomy

ORDER: *Anoplura* (sucking lice)
FAMILY: *Pediculidae*
GENUS AND SPECIES: *Pediculus humanus* (head lice)

Parasites of caterpillars

Many species of wasps in the families Ichneumonidae and Braconidae are parasites. Female ichneumons and braconids lay their eggs on the larvae of other insects. Many choose a particular species of caterpillar. Some have extremely long ovipositors that can push through plant stems, galls, or tree bark, reaching larvae that are tunneling inside. When the wasp eggs hatch, the wasp larvae begin developing inside the body of their host. The host continues to live for a time. Some even pupate and emerge as adults. Eventually, however, the maturing wasps kill their hosts. You may find caterpillars with tiny wasp cocoons attached to their bodies, or dead, dry caterpillars or cocoons with ichneumons or braconids pupating inside. Some wasps parasitize caterpillars that feed on food crops, and in this way are helpful to farmers and gardeners.

55

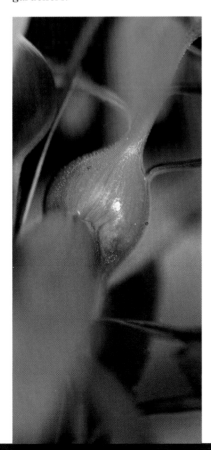

Taxonomy

ORDER: *Hymenoptera (ants, bees, and wasps)*
FAMILIES: *Ichneumonidae and Braconidae*

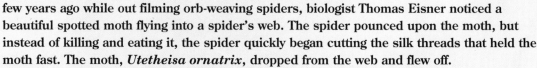

FIELD TRIP | DISCOVERIES

A few years ago while out filming orb-weaving spiders, biologist Thomas Eisner noticed a beautiful spotted moth flying into a spider's web. The spider pounced upon the moth, but instead of killing and eating it, the spider quickly began cutting the silk threads that held the moth fast. The moth, *Utetheisa ornatrix*, dropped from the web and flew off.

His curiosity aroused, Eisner tried to offer Utetheisa to other spiders and insect-eating birds. None would have it! Eisner suspected that the moth was chemically protected, that is, some substance in its body repelled predators. Adult Utetheisa occasionally drink nectar, but Utetheisa caterpillars feed on plants in the genus Crotalaria. These plants contain poisonous chemicals called pyrrolizidine alkaloids. Do alkaloids accumulate in the larvae and remain in their bodies when they metamorphose into adults? And are they responsible for the fact that predators refuse to eat Utetheisa? Eisner and his colleagues devised some experiments to help them find out.

In the Lab

Following up a discovery

Eisner and his colleagues decided to see if predators treated alkaloid-free moths any differently than moths with alkaloids in their bodies. But first, they had to find a way to raise alkaloid-free moths. They fed the caterpillars a special diet based on pinto beans. One group of caterpillars was raised on a plain, alkaloid-free version of this diet, while another was given the bean diet with seeds from Crotalaria mixed in. A third group of Utetheisa was collected from the field where, in all likelihood, they had been eating Crotalaria. The researchers dropped caterpillars and moths from each group in front of spiders. The spiders promptly grabbed, then began to eat those raised on the plain bean diet. They rejected the other two groups.

It was clear that eating Crotalaria offered caterpillars and moths protection from spiders, but were the pyrrolizidine alkaloids really responsible? To check, the researchers took pure alkaloids from Crotalaria and added these chemicals to bits of food. Then, they offered the food to spiders. The spiders refused to eat items contaminated with alkaloids, which convinced Eisner and his team that these chemicals were, in fact, protecting Utetheisa from predators.

How could the spiders tell that their food had been poisoned? The morsels the researchers offered them did not look like spotted moths. And, what prompted spiders in the wild to free any Utetheisa they caught in their webs? In the dark, the bright colors of these moths don't show up well, and orb-web builders aren't known for their eyesight anyway! Most likely, taste tipped them off. When a spider first touches its prey, sensors on its legs and palps pick up chemical information, much as the taste buds on our tongues do. Spiders quickly reject food containing poisonous alkaloids after they've inspected it. Probably, it just doesn't taste good to them.

57

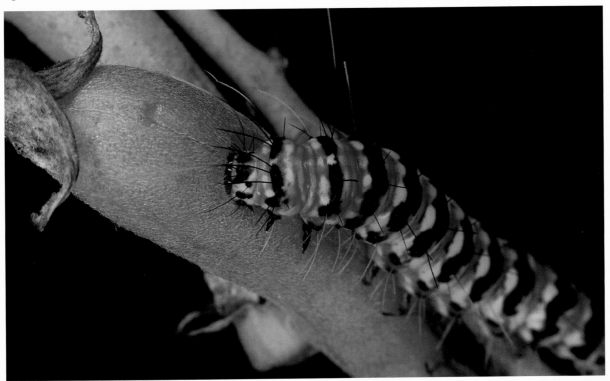

Insect Migration

Many insects live in parts of the world where seasonal cold weather makes it difficult to move or find food. Most overwinter as eggs or pupae, but a few make regular journeys called **migrations**. Some milkweed bugs fly south for the winter, and many lady beetles fly up into the mountains. Certain butterflies, locusts, and dragonflies also migrate.

Migrating monarchs

Monarch butterflies that emerge in early or midsummer do not travel far. They feed, mate, and produce another generation of caterpillars near the place where they were hatched. But those that emerge at the end of summer do something entirely different. After their wings are dry, they begin an amazing migration. Some fly from just west of the Rocky Mountains to the coast of California. Others fly from eastern Canada and the United States all the way to the mountains of south-central Mexico. Their delicate wings carry them thousands of miles! They stop along the way to feed, and to rest at night in trees, but they do not stop for long until they have reached the trees where they will spend the winter. When winter ends, they will mate and begin the long flight back.

Monarchs from northern areas probably don't fly all the way back to the places where they were hatched. Instead, they lay eggs and die in more southerly parts of their range. Their offspring, when mature, continue the journey northward. It may take several generations of travelers to reach the same northern areas that migrants left the previous fall.

Why migrate?

The places where monarchs spend the winter might surprise you. In the mountain forests of Mexico, for example, winter temperatures are usually above freezing, but still chilly. Overwintering monarchs cling to the bark and branches of trees, unable to fly except on the warmest days. Monarchs do not migrate to lands of warmth and food where they can remain active all winter, as many migratory birds do. Instead, they fly thousands of miles in order to cling to a cold tree. Why?

Scientists think that these chilly temperatures may actually benefit monarchs by preventing them from flying and burning up their body fat. Of course, they can't stay in a place that is really cold; temperatures below freezing would kill them. Cold enough to save energy, but warm enough to live—that's the secret.

A recent discovery, and many more questions

Until 1975, no one was sure where the eastern monarchs spent the winter. It took persistent researchers and volunteers, both adults and children, decades to discover their wintering grounds in Mexico. There are still many mysteries that scientists are trying to unravel. How do migrating monarchs know where to go? Do they use either the earth's magnetic field or the sun to help them navigate? What determines where a spring migrant will stop to lay eggs, and what determines which eggs will hatch into migrants and which into monarchs that stay put?

An endangered phenomenon

Though many important aspects of monarch migration were discovered only recently, and many questions remain, the phenomenon of monarch migration is one that may not always be here to observe. Even though the monarchs' wintering grounds themselves have been left alone, development and foresting near those areas are changing environmental conditions within. Cutting the forest around a colony may cause temperatures inside it to fluctuate more widely than the monarchs can tolerate, killing many butterflies. People concerned about this problem are trying to protect the butterflies, while appreciating the economic needs of people who live and work near the monarchs' wintering grounds.

Getting Rid of Insects:

© BILL IVY

A t times insect pests merely annoy us. Other times they pose more serious problems. Some insects are **carriers** of diseases that infect people and other animals. Other insects trouble us by damaging our buildings and food crops. It's not surprising that people have sought efficient, economical ways to dispose of damage-causing insects.

Pesticides

Pesticides are chemicals used to kill unwanted plants or animals. **Insecticides** are those pesticides specifically designed to get rid of insects. Both are widely used in many countries. City dwellers may employ an exterminator on a regular basis in hopes of keeping cockroaches at bay, while people in rural areas dust crops and spray orchards with insecticides to protect their harvest. In the suburbs, weed killers and other poisons are used to keep lawns neat and green. Some pesticides have been in use for many years, while others are relatively new.

The DDT story

The more we use pesticides, the more we learn about their effects. Most of them cause problems as well as solve them. **DDT** is a well-known example. DDT (short for dichlorodiphenyltrichloroethane) was first introduced in the 1940s to combat a variety of insect pests.

It was applied to agricultural land to kill crop-eating insects, to trees to slow the spread of Dutch elm disease, and to water to kill mosquito eggs and larvae. In some places it was sprayed on walls to kill flies and mosquitoes that landed there. It was even sprayed directly on people!

DDT helped reduce the incidence of typhus, malaria, and other insect-borne diseases in many parts of the world, and it increased agricultural production in others. But during the 1950s and 1960s, many people became concerned about its side effects. It killed "non-target" insect species, including beneficial predators and pollinators, as well as the pests it was intended to eliminate. Birds and other animals that ate insects contaminated with DDT were also poisoned. Though these problems had been somewhat anticipated, living with them made many people question the widespread use of DDT.

Surprising long-term effects of DDT began to show up as well. Scientists discovered that DDT was slow to break down into harmless chemicals. Instead of eliminating it in their waste, insects stored it up in their fatty tissue. Small fish, songbirds, and other insect-eaters consumed DDT whenever they preyed on contaminated insects. They in

The Problem of Pesticides

turn stored the poison in their fatty tissue and passed it along to larger fish, hawks, and other predators that ate them. DDT did not kill these predators outright, but it had other serious effects. Birds of prey, like the osprey, began to lay eggs with thin, easily broken shells. Most of these eggs did not hatch, and few young birds matured to replace older ones that died. Along the northeastern coast, efforts to remove mosquitoes from the marshes nearly eliminated the osprey instead.

The environmental damage caused by DDT brought the complicated issue of pest control to public attention, and in 1972 DDT was banned in the United States.

Alternatives to chemical pesticides

For as long as people have been raising crops, they have found ways to control pest insects. Caterpillars can be picked off of food plants by hand, and insect eggs can be crushed. The trouble with these simple, direct methods of control is that they are time-consuming.

Other alternatives to pesticides exist. Some farmers and gardeners stock their plantings with **predaceous** insects, such as praying mantids, that will hunt crop-eating insects. Others spray crops with microorganisms that infect insects with fatal diseases. Like chemical pesticides, these methods are not **species specific**; praying mantids will eat a wide variety of insects, not just pest species. However, they are unlikely to lead to the kind of widespread environmental damage associated with chemicals like DDT.

Recovering

In the early 1970s researchers imported osprey eggs from places that had been less contaminated with DDT to nests along the northeast coast, where the osprey population had crashed. The uncontaminated eggs hatched, and the young birds eventually mated and raised young of their own in their new homeland. Together with the DDT ban, this program allowed a seriously threatened osprey population to recover.

Continuing

Professional entomologists often collaborate with one another. Working together, they can learn from each other's expertise, and discuss new ideas. You can track down people in your area who are interested in insects. They may be able to answer questions you might have, and they will help you keep going!

People to contact

It's fun to have company when you observe or collect. Your friends or classmates may have experience finding and raising insects that they can share with you.

Ask if any teachers at your school are particularly interested in insects. If there is a college, university, or research center near you, call to find out if there are any entomologists, biologists, or ecologists on staff who can either meet

with you or answer questions by phone. Check the phone book to see if there is a nature center or museum in your area. Some museums have collections of living or preserved specimens that you can look at. **Curators** who take care of these collections, may help you identify a specimen, or provide tips on insect care.

Does your community have a county agent? County agents are often up-to-date on local insects, particularly pest species.

Many gardeners also know a great deal about the insects that visit their flowers and vegetables. They may be happy to have you collect eggs and caterpillars from their plants to take home and raise.

How to Order Specimens and Supplies

You'll have more fun if you collect the specimens you need and build the equipment yourself. But microscopes and nets are hard to build. And sometimes it's difficult to find live specimens depending on the season and your location. Many cities have stores that sell scientific equipment. Check your yellow pages under Science, Hobby, or Microscopes.

Almost all of the equipment and specimens mentioned in *Entomology* can be ordered through the mail or by phone at reasonable prices from a company called Carolina Biological Supply. If you want to order by phone, you'll need an adult with a credit card. A handling charge is added to each order.

EASTERN U.S.
Carolina Biological Supply
2700 York Road
Burlington, NC 27215
Toll free 1-800-334-5551

WESTERN U.S.
Carolina Biological Supply
Box 187
Gladstone, OR 97027
Toll free 1-800-547-1733

Please remember: If you order live specimens, make sure you have everything you need to feed and house them before they arrive. Instructions are often included with any equipment or live insects you order from a biological supply house. If you have further questions about your order, call the company since they are in the business of rearing certain species of insects.

First of all, you need an insect net and a magnifier (pages 8-9). Carolina Biological Supply has a Pacific Aerial Net for approximately $15 which will do nicely, and a Thermo-Plastic Magnifier, 4X, for about $1. If you have a hard time finding caterpillars to raise (pages 16-17) you can order a Painted Lady Butterfly Kit for about $12 from Carolina. It includes a rearing chamber, 3 to 5 larvae, and

food. Aquatic Nets (pages 18-19) are kind of expensive (Carolina has one for about $23). Unless you live near a pond, it's probably not worth it. Damselfly Nymphs and Dragonfly Nymphs (pages 20-21) cost about $16 for 12, but they're not available in winter. You'll probably be able to capture your own live crickets (pages 22-23), but you can order 12 House Cricket Adults for about $6, or a "Little Chirper" Cricket Cage, which comes with a cage, six live crickets, and food for about $12. Twelve Milkweed Bug Adults (pages 28-29) cost about $10, as do enough Milkweed Bug Eggs to start a colony. If you order milkweed bugs, also order Milkweed Bug Food (about $4) which they have been bred to eat instead of milkweed. Carolina also sells a Milkweed Bug Culture Kit for about $25, which includes eggs, food, a container, watering vial, climbing mat, and instructions. Carolina sells a Styrofoam Insect Mounting Board (pages 44-45) with a variable center groove for about $20. Anti-rust Insect Pins cost about $8 for a package of 100, and a Cardboard Insect Box costs about $11 (though you can probably improvise one yourself). Microscopes (pages 48-49) can be very expensive. For the purposes of this book, a hand lens is adequate, and if you want to get a little more ambitious you can order a 10X Miniscope from Carolina for about $24. It has a light source, batteries included, and is small enough to be used in the field as well as at home.

ATTENTION TEACHERS: *Most of the equipment and specimens are available at quantity discounts for classroom use. In addition to Carolina Biological Supply, these supplies are also available from Science Kit and Boreal Laboratories (1-800-828-7777) and Wards Natural Science Establishment (1-800-962-2660).*

Glossary

abdomen: the segmented hind section of an insect's body that contains the reproductive organs.

aerate: to expose to air, or to bubble air into a liquid.

aestivate: to spend time in an unmoving state during a period of hot or dry weather.

alar spot: a small, black spot on each hind wing of a male monarch butterfly.

Animalia: the animal kingdom.

Annelida: the phylum of segmented worms.

Anoplura: the insect order that includes the head lice and body lice that parasitize humans.

anther: on a flower, the part of the stamen that contains the pollen.

aquatic: living in water.

Arachnoidea: the class of animals that includes spiders.

Arthropoda: the phylum that includes spiders, lobsters, insects, and many other animals with jointed legs.

carnivore: an animal-eater.

carrier: an animal that picks up germs or parasites from one animal and transports them to another.

caste: a sub-group within a colony of social insects.

cerci: abdominal appendages on some insects that pick up information about the surrounding environment.

chemically protected: a function of some insects' bodies that protects them from predators by producing or concentrating chemicals that repel would-be predators.

Chilopoda: centipedes and their relatives.

chrysalis: the pupal stage of a butterfly.

class: a group of living things. Taxonomists put closely related species together in the same genus, related genera into a family, related families into the same order, and related orders into the same class.

Coleoptera: the insect order that contains the beetles.

complete metamorphosis: a type of insect development characterized by egg, larva, pupa, and adult stages.

cremaster: the "stem" that holds a monarch chrysalis.

crop: on a bee's body, a storage chamber for storing and transporting swallowed food.

cross-pollination: the transfer of pollen from the anther of one flower to the stigma of another flower.

Crustacea: a class of animals with jointed legs, exoskeletons, and two pairs of antennae.

curator: a person in charge of a museum, zoo, or other place of exhibit.

DDT: an insecticide once used heavily in the United States, but now prohibited because of the environmental damage it caused.

Dermaptera: the insect order that includes earwigs.

detritivore: an organism that eats detritus.

detritus: fragments of organic matter, such as bits of decaying plants and animals.

diapause: an unmoving state in which some insects spend the winter.

Diplopoda: millipedes and their relatives.

Diptera: the insect order that includes flies, mosquitoes, gnats, and their relatives.

domestic insect: any of various insects that are used and raised by people, such as honeybees.

dormant: inactive; resting

drone: a male wasp or bee.

elytra: the hard or leathery forewings of an adult beetle.

entomology: the study of insects.

evolve: to change over time through a process called evolution.

exit holes: tiny holes on a gall that indicate that the origional inhabitant has chewed its way out and moved on.

exoskeleton: a hard, outside body covering that protects internal organs and serves as a place for muscles to attach to.

family: a group of living things. A number of related genera form a family.

genus: a group of related species.

gill chamber: a structure within a dragonfly nymph's abdomen, used to extract oxygen from the water.

glycosides: chemicals found in milkweed plants.

gradual metamorphosis (also called incomplete metamorphosis): a type of insect development characterized by egg, nymph, and adult stages.

head: the part of an insect's body bearing the eyes, antennae, and mouthparts.

Hemiptera: the insect order that contains the true bugs.

herbivore: a plant-eater.

hierarchy: in a colony of insects, the organized rank of individual insects.

Homoptera: the insect order that contains cicadas, leafhoppers, aphids, and their relatives.

honeycomb: wax cells built by bees for storing honey, and housing eggs and developing young.

honeydew: a sweet deposit secreted on the leaves of plants, usually by aphids.

host: an organism with one or more parasites living on or in it.

Hymenoptera: the insect order that includes bees, wasps, and ants.

imago: a newly-emerged adult insect.

immunity: resistance to illness or infection.

induce: to cause by influence or stimulation.

Insecta: the large class of animals commonly called insects.

insecticide: a chemical used to kill insect pests.

instar: the stage between molts.

introduced species: an organism that is transported to an area that is not its native environment.

Isoptera: the insect order that includes termites.

jointed legs: legs with a number of segments. Two segments meet at a joint.

kingdom: a group of living things. Scientists group all living things into several large divisions, or kingdoms.

larvae: an early stage in the life cycle of some animals. Insects with complete metamorphosis have larvae.

Lepidoptera: the insect order that contains moths and butterflies.

metamorphosis: a physical change of form some animals undergo as they develop.

migrations: regular, seasonal journeys.

mimic: an organism that looks similar to a different species.

mimicry: a natural phenomenon wherein some species closely resemble others.

molt: to shed the exoskeleton, or skin.

mutualism: a relationship between two organisms that benefits both.

nectar: a sweet liquid produced by flowers, and used by bees to make honey.

nymph: the young of any insect with gradual metamorphosis.

Odonata: the insect order that includes dragonflies and damselflies.

omnivore: an organism that eats both plants and animals.

order: a group of living things. A number of related families comprise an order.

Orthoptera: the insect order that includes crickets, grasshoppers, cockroaches, mantids, and others.

overwinter: to spend the winter.

ovipositor: an anatomical feature used to deposit eggs.

palps: small, feeler-like structures near the mouth of some insects.

parthenogenesis: reproduction without fertilization of the egg.

pest: a species that annoys people, or causes harm to food crops or property.

pesticide: a chemical used to kill unwanted plants or animals.

phylum: a group of animals, and the primary divisions in the animal kingdom.

pollen baskets: hairy segments on the legs of some bees, that hold pollen.

pollinate: to transfer pollen from anther to stigma.

predaceous: to live by capturing and eating other animals.

proboscis: a long, straw-like mouthpart.

protective coloration: coloring that makes an animal difficult to see against a particular background, and serves as protection from predators.

pupal stage: in complete metamorphosis, the stage of development between larvae and imago, usually occurring within a cocoon or chrysalis.

pyrrolizidine alkaloids: chemicals found in plants in the genus *Crotalaria*.

queen: a reproductive female in a colony of social wasps, ants, termites, or bees. Often, there is just one queen per colony.

reproductive potential: the capacity to produce offspring.

segmented body: an animal's body, composed of a number of similar sections.

smoking: the process of introducing smoke to a beehive, usually to calm bees so that honey can be collected.

social insects: insects that live together in groups, or colonies. Each member of a colony works to help the whole group survive.

solitary insect: living alone; not a social insect.

species: divisions within a genus of distinct kinds of organisms. Members of the same species can mate and produce more organisms like themselves.

species specific: relating to just one species. This term is often used to describe pesticides, parasites, and disease organisms.

spiracles: openings on the surface of an insect's body that are part of its breathing system. They connect to internal air passageways.

stigma: on a flower, the tip of the pistil, and the place where pollen must fall if fruit and seeds are to develop.

swarm: a mass of flying insects. Also a large group of bees, including a queen, that has left the hive in search of a new place to live.

taxonomy: classification.

terrestrial: living on land.

territorial: having to do with a given area, or territory. A territorial insect may try to keep intruders away from a particular place.

thorax: the midsection of an insect's body, bearing legs and/or wings.

Trichoptera: the insect order that contains the caddisflies.

ventral: the "belly" side, or underside, of an animal.

worker: a non-reproductive member of a colony of social insects. Workers find food, construct and repair the hive or nest, and tend to the queen.